That Time I Wrote My Life In Poetry

Lia P

with Illustrations by Kevin Palmer

ISBN: 0998193194
ISBN-13: 978-0998193199

DEDICATION

This work is dedicated to my Good Girlfriends.

"Poetry is what my writing looks like when I am unapologetically honest."

Lia P

Table of Contents

ACKNOWLEDGMENTS

I thank my ancestors and all of my
Good Girlfriends.

Good Girlfriends

Good girlfriends know before you
it's over with him
Walk you to cramped bathroom at hospital when
healthy baby debuts
Hold your head while you defecate
the too much you did that night
Rock your children while you say goodbye
to baby who won't be born
Pack boxes from office you sat in
when you played grownup corporate games
Shop for jeans with you at Ross
after platinum card closes
Tackle goddess braids in hair
with fatigued fingers
Listen to tears and conversations absent of hair
Read all your written pieces
and claim they are brilliant
Never mention pounds or pimples
Let you fantasize about singlehood
Buy you Tiffany jewelry and Kate Spade pumps
Don't ask for receipts
Ever
They love you
through everything

SOME STUFF I WROTE AS A CHILD

My Wish
(written in the early 80s)

If I had one wish
You know what it would be
To crawl inside of you
And take your misery

To see the things you see
To feel all that you feel
To know what's in your heart
To make your dreams turn real

I'd care for you best inside
My love would fill your heart
I'd grab another wish
That we should never part

The Make-up Artist
(1986)

She wore a sensual beauty
Her only love lured by her grace
Those who dare to look upon her
Dazzled by colors in her face

The enemy of pulchritude
This artist tried to defeat
But the vital gift was soon lost
To the close clutch of evil heat

The death of possessed perfection
Would produce a silent tone
No longer would her love exist
She must conquer life alone

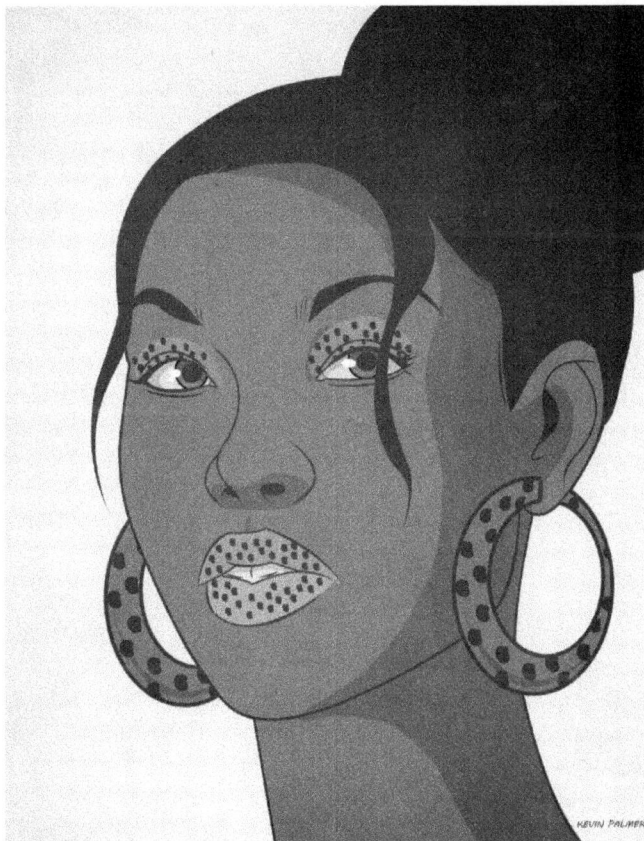

a child's poem for adults

a tear can be a spice
the salt tastes rather nice
a tear can be a friend
its warmness from within
a tear can clear up dirt
or wash a messy shirt
a tear can release pain
it doesn't cause much strain
a tear can cleanse your eye
it's quite okay to cry

the voice of a forgotten child
(1985, Previously published in the Loyola *Cadence*
Magazine)

A desolate, dreary, dismal world is my home
Awaiting the time when I will be moribund
My life not my own
Misread, neglected, and despondent am I
My end predicted
Soon I must die
A face pallid with fear
Belongs to me
My only possession
Will never be free
A place that would be warm
Is suddenly cold
My future dire
My story untold
A voice unheard, unloved, untouched
Is mine
For it is only the voice of a dying mind

The Power of a Smile

A smile is a homemade apple pie
It's inviting and tempting
A smile is a crisp, cool morning
It's fresh and new
A smile is a soft symphony
It's pleasant and comforting
A smile is a common cold
It's sometimes contagious
A smile is a box of plush tissues
It's able to wipe away tears
A smile is a beautiful bouquet of flowers
It's pretty and colorful
A smile is a thick, heavy blanket
It's warm and affectionate
A smile is your favorite meal cooking
It's always waiting for you to enjoy

STUFF I WROTE LATER

A Note to My Ex

Last winter

I shed hair

I shed skin

I shed you

Mama

when the pain of my past
formed coral-colored clouds
you became my eyes
when dreams danced
too far from reach
you lifted me upon your stern shoulder to catch
them
when fear tried to command my fate
you bravely fought each attempt
when my eyes filled with salted wells
your hands cupped the moisture
when puddles streamed at my feet
you taught me to love the reflection below

Clouds

Do they know they are despair metaphor
Though children splash in their pools
Cool in their mist
Form them into animals and super heroes

Lyrics, letters and poems exploit them
Never acknowledging their worth
Effortlessly doing their job
Protecting the earth

Anthem

Crawl space in cages
confuses confinement with freedom.
Nonplus pores call ancestors for redemption
while locked doors block pathways to progress.
The rock of hope cries to crack the combination.
Her beauty barren by man's anemic trophies.
Her strength weakened by our walls of senility.
Sleeping through the sonance of our vinculum,
we fight fake wars on blood-bathed land.
Sharp wounds penetrate lightly,
though poison permeates.
Bones bake in sunlight's oven.
Historians spin nightmares into repugnant utopias.
Our damaged dialects steal breaths while drowning.
The glare of titanium bars blinds its captors.
Caffeine comforts our imperative confusion
as we build death on foreign soil.

Dorothy
(written in 1998)

Eyes
dark, round radio dials,
stuck on the am station of past.

Fatal figure sunk in thin hospital mattress.
Counts days she might last.

She is one in ten.

One in ten
Los Angeles earth-dyed glories,
Santa Monica beach water blue
draped on flawless figures,
tresses teased in rainbow flips,
mouths dipped in shades of fetish and ooh baby
gloss,
swing motherland mating calls
to Talib beats.

Lose friends, family, forthcoming fantasies.

Meet past in hell.

Fire singes follicles to brain.
Immune deficient to healing of ancestors.

Buried Dorothy.

20-something choices a noose around her neck.
Tubes make the umbilical cord impossible to

connect.
Glittered shoes too loose to blow her back home
and all the brick roads paved with time bombs.

Earth sucks bones into orifice of its skin.
Blood veins matriculate to death.
Mirror reflects new-formed cover of caked bruises.

Devoured Dorothy
could have been me.

Nightclubs with friends.
Places I should not have been.
I could have been
one in ten.

If her insides could talk
her cells off the ledge of the building,
miracles would fall instead of cadavers.

Dorothy an angel beating on my eardrum.
Dorothy an angel beating on my eardrum.
Dorothy an angel beating on my eardrum.

A prayer I sent to God.

And I
brown blessing in the nine.

Irreparable

Neither calla lilies nor carnations at gravesite.

Negro hymns,
euro centric religion,
fetal in bellies.

Oceans of sad.
Skin baked yams beneath surface.
Aborted riches
breeds barren homeland.

A microwave memory removal
will not heal
the gaping hole torn into the gut of my history.

Chemicals can't eradicate the kinkiness of my
ancestral ambiguity.

Rinsing guilt in reparations
while the lie is reincarnated.

Race is Fiction written to contain and contaminate.

Coins will not cure the contradictions we've
become.

Leaving our blackness in the hands of an Ethiopian
braider on Crenshaw.
Aligning ourselves with indentured lyricists
as somehow nigga sounds slightly more soothing

slipping from their lips.

Even I get distracted by the rhythm of my early
childhood
the part I'm told to forfeit for its absence of
designer appliances.

Feebly attempting to re-identify myself with no
viable leads to my genealogy.

Attached to the black Buddha encased at the
Smithsonian.
PYRAMIDS constructed in Southern Africa
as my face bears no resemblance to Egyptians and
the use of that region has become trite.

We protest separatism
yet claim races on applications and census forms.

Enslave ourselves in the chains
of acquiring superficial success.

While the compound interest of our self-hatred
increases daily.

I Designed You

let my tears
be the blood in your veins
placed my future in your hands
for you to grind like coffee beans
watched you pick the remnants
from your fingernails
to dissipate like dust in wind
placed my heart at your feet
to walk into coarse ground
wrapped my happiness in you
to shred
fell deep into your pool of deception
and never surfaced.

Reflections of my Soul
(1992)

I paint my visage prudently
A contrived joy which radiates and reflects
Perfection
Dancing off the luminous colors in my mind

I keep pain at a comfortable distance
Feelings coated in anxiety
Standing defiantly in judgment of those
Foolish enough to take chances on muscles and
mustaches

Tears fall violently in secret puddles
They fill bowls of abandonment, rejection and
loneliness
My choices often limited
To suitors who abhor me
As I do

Life has not bestowed me with beauty
My mirror resonates thunderously
The tune of my imperfections & inadequacies
To all other sounds

I am DEAF

THAT TIME I WROTE MY LIFE IN POETRY

Witness

Don't think I don't hear
the pain in your voice
coffee brown brother
void of choice
Your dreams melt like butter
abandoned in heat
the pools of your tears
cover my feet
Don't think I don't feel
your manhood shrink
the red, hot fire
fade to pink
Your slick, slow stride
turned to a crawl
my hands reach below
to catch your fall
Don't think I don't know
you were born to be king
slaves still rape your land
for the sake of a ring
Fear has transcended
and ghettoized your throne
Don't think, my brother,
you're here alone.

On Being FREE
(1987, Previously published in the Loyola *Cadence* Magazine)

The verdict is decided.
I am jailed in a free world;
Bars of self-hatred
Bricks of self-destruction
CONVICTED
By prejudice
with ignorance as the only evidence

"Give him 50 or 60 years
Give him til' infinity
to learn to LOVE the color BLACK."

Enraged is my mind
For it struggles with my heart

"They" gave me the emancipation
But I am still bound
And I must thank them for letting me
Acquire financial status
My success has made me rich?
My BLACKness is still poor

Because

It has no soul
And
A color with no pride
Is an icy-cold heart

"They" carry on about "freedoms" granted to me
As if they should not have been mine
Since the beginning of time!
Blinded by their desire to find answers
For imperfect world
I AM BLAMED
While in the deepest regions of my SOUL
I cry out like a roaring tiger
In the BLACKest forest

When will I be FREE?

Fantasy

I pretend nails stuck in his feet
Like Jesus
So he can't leave
The baby boy
Dribbling yesterday's cinnamon oatmeal down his
flabby chin
And the girl
Hair like exposed wire
Or the veins of an unlucky gambler
Whose debtors claimed skin for payment

I am southern granny
A Salem sorceress
Mystic potion oozing from pores
I make those other women cod liver oil

Me, a conductor
Direct mama and daddy to touch like they still in
high school
Like they have no past
Like the last book in the bible

But he rips from nails
She slips and wounds her ability to care
Us babies play tag circling her forever
Our spirit has walked out

Brothers

Brothers love deeply
Though they slide by looking cool
They weep in secret

Love

Love is a labor
Is my paycheck in the mail
I worked overtime

Reminisce

it must have been beautiful once
like the last day of middle school
or the first time he called
it had to be
at some point
at least
nice
because I was soldered to him
And only GOD could remove me.

Nameless

She's pregnant again
Long black braids scratch her backside
Stomach protruding
Breasts drooping
Surly yet susceptible to her mother's crack habit
Panties bleed black
from bruises dealers sent her in brown packages
UPS didn't track
Fourteen years young, neatly donned in daddy's
neglect
Trades boys for men
Plays hide and go f--
Does the nasty in her Winnie the Pooh nightgown
High heel hickies in her throat
She grows old
Rapid
Like Michael Jordan's air
Waits for despondent SAT scores to judge her
Counselors guide her to failure
So she craves hoop dreams
as her first baby screams
scratches, scrawls gang signs in his bassinet
Burns dinner
Fills womb with foul smells of
blackened chicken over chronic
I try to save her standing steadfast on my lofty
soapbox
But I get lost in ghettoes
And she needs a better guide
Un-perplexed by circuitous routes

I pray
I cry
My bleeding heart not enough
Her life is tough
like leaving good sex
like driving in snow with no four-wheel drive
I wish I were her answer
Not a spectator
injured in the first quarter
Sitting, silent on sidelines
as she moves further from my grasp
lecherous lies, linger long and sleep in her bed
I visit weakly but my medicine is Western
her reaction allergic
She's fourteen years young and pregnant
Reprieve at Disneyland no fun ride
Her head shakes with each rumble of gang fire
and empty intervention
and pipelined relatives
Fetus growls for substance
buried before birth
in blanket
of fabricated.

OLD S@#t

Got some old s@#t
Old lyrics to old songs
I'm stepping in old s@#t and it's
Stuck on my shoe
Funky and heavy and reminds me of you
Your old words
You wrote to those old tunes
Kept re-opening old wounds
You sang me each morning
Your words piercing
So I purged them
Purposefully
And as I defecated my dysfunction
You periodically crept, snuck, stole
Parts of me
that still reek
With that old s@#t.

Be Like
(written in the 90's)

Black boys with no daddies
Be like pancakes with no Bisquick
Be like collards with no salt pork
Be like Cleveland with no blizzards
Be like music with no rhythm
Be like Christmas with no happy
Be like drugs with no White House
Be like immigrants with no faith
Be like love with no pain
Be like Chi-town with no house jams
Be like candy with no sweet
Be like sun with no warmth
Be like Africa with no Mandela
Be like America with no racism
Be like sisters with no bootys
Be like brothers with no cool
Be like rap songs with no anger
Be like jazz with no soul
Be like day with no night
Be like poetry with no words
Black boys with no daddies
Be like me with no you.

Phyllis's Aria

She floated to the croon of Cab and Ella.
Captivating suitors, swinging her swanky hips.
Charming cherubs, from the ruby red of her lips.
Diamonds competed with her brilliance.
Love songs, letters, long walks on the moon.
She rolled dice in the grocer's alley to select her
soul mate groom.
Perfumed of collards and cornbread.
Her kitchen a symphony conducted with love.
Fastidious, feisty.
Even at eighty, her tango tamed troubles.
She danced with her man on the ocean.
Light feet leaped often to distant shores.
An uninvited visitor arrived at her door.
She refused to let him in.
He took her husband while she slept.
She wept.
She waited.
She danced with him again.

Bad Habits

routinely, i brush my hair and teeth
and love men who ain't no good for me,
get angry
when they follow
my lucid instructions
laid easy on their beds
the way I do.

Kevin Palmer

Pop Pop

They called him Joseph in pool halls
where he wore his screaming red jacket,
black and white loafers,
with an occasional cigar
leaning on his bottom lip.
Joseph was his name
when his mouth nearly got him hung in Tennessee,
when he whipped mommy up a pine tree
and served cocktails to the mob to feed his family.
But he was Pop Pop to me
because he placed a dozen roses at my door,
carried pictures of my childhood in his hip pocket
and laughed like a newborn being tickled when I
called.
No brown bags of money ever passed through my
door
just Pop Pop's smile.

My Earliest Memory of Him

he sucked on baby cigarettes
circling our living room
in a cloud of funk and fervor
eyes glued glazed
to passing days
passing friends
and passing battles he fought
for unidentified causes
eyes periodically poured us
glimpse of happy

the missing ingredient
in mom's homemade sweet rolls
neither her Avon perfume or steadfast persistence
could remove the stain
of dead cousins on his narrow feet

death remained, rested with him each night
stayed trapped, trembling in his head
his muted heart
speech impaired
looted by denied rights
and leaders who now lived on street signs

letters came when he left
but only quiet visited when he returned
and filled our home
with daddy's baby mushroom clouds
dampening the weight
of what he never said

Everett
(2002)

First name too ordinary to wear
Buried with war scars and boyhood bruises he don't
expose
Walk like he birthed cool
Love to talk s…
Puffing a…cigar
Exhale staccato with measured belly laugh

Navigate his ride on ice through chi-town hawk
Forehead swell primary colors when wronged in
suburban fast food line
where wrinkled Jewish ladies
clutch past

Like dependable things
vamp red Volvo
city with four seasons
buckeye trees blooming for attention
children who feed on fables
with ballooned ached bellies on movie Saturday
Marcia

Daddy be Real Cool
like a Cleveland Christmas
Malcolm X oration
Miles Davis movement
Daddy be Real Cool…

Confirmation

Twelve
Doused in salmon silk
Monstrous lace
Camouflaging tomboy scrapes and gestures
Shoes glisten like the barrel of my first curling iron
Limbs like pool sticks daddy used to collect quick
cash in college
Snickering while mommy clasps the hands of round
nuns
A true believer
Enamored by the lingered creases of folds from
mornings to nights
Burying her wooden crucifix in the goose pillow
Lighting lavender candles at lent to heal broken
promises

With her in the over-dressed cathedral
Sunlight does back flips down the aisle
Slaps my calves
The aged, oak pews fill with stoic faces
Rising, sitting by rote
Entranced by Latin litanies

My brother unwraps banana now and laters
Slips them under seat
I am woman now
But I have childish needs
Like candy
And piggyback rides
From my missing father

My eyes dart about
Seeking his figure
Missing me walk taller

I imagine him at the home my mother inherited
from the divorce
Babysitting my cassata cake, vanilla ice cream, an
enveloped stuffed full of crisp bills

But he is there
Stuck on that street
Hammered against his gasping garnet Volvo
Betrayed by the frayed sidewalk that only vaguely
recognizes him
Soiled by officers who feed on cheap cigars
And prospect prostitutes

No path through our front door
No evidence he belongs inside
Cops cannot see
I have his eyes
And mommy's fear of abandonment
He belongs in that house
Even with no key.

Saturdays

i sat on the third concrete step
in a Cleveland suburb
whose theme song was silence
where children rallied to the buzz of fireflies
kicked buckeyes into cracks
and boomed george clinton at block parties

saturdays i sat
wishing,
with baby brother
squishing lady bugs beneath feet
daring yellow jackets to approach
beneath white french windows
married to our brick house

and daddy scooped us up on saturdays
often late
always welcomed
us skipping to his Christmas red Volvo
singing happy
to cedar point or king's island
for candied apples and sugared sleep
fluorescent green necklaces
roller coaster dips

my stomach still aches from the ride

Sitting Between Us

Aching words we shoot
with our semi-automatic mouths
Lies we use as sheets of emotional protection
Contaminated cloud of my past
Divestment from us to invest in the newness
of others
Cumbersome expectations
of the friends and family audience
Contaminated cloud of our wrong doings
The torn pieces of our relationship
Sitting in between us

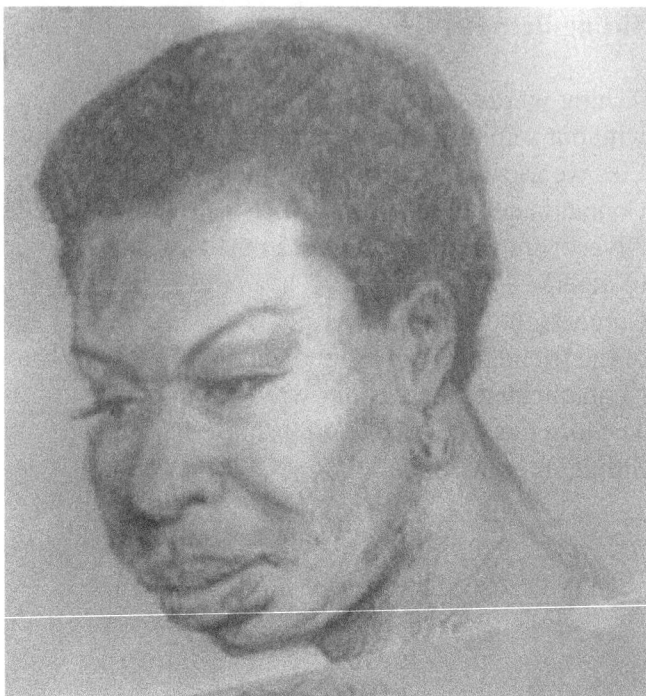

Open

Cancun
Canvas of sunbathed beaches
Beer soaked bars
Sunflowers, marigolds, Mexican sage
Crashing against Crayola blue green backgrounds
Breed jalapeno thoughts
Your spirit etched in ruins
I climb seeking solace
From boys poorly posturing as men
Hands rocking crotches to paralysis
In jazz festival mac stance
Mispronouncing music legend names
Crafting decayed first impression
Oil from box braids blend with cocoa butter back
Hoodoo potion in my fleshy folds
I dance concheros mating call
Tequila truth on your breath
Your name henna on my heart
You, pacific ocean breeze
Baby tender
First love open
We black unity
Cry freedom chants
El chicon volcano
Tender chicken tamale dreams
Me full
Feasting on your image
Jetting home in Mexicana's 6th row

STUFF I WROTE MORE RECENTLY

Black Autism

Smells like prison pipeline
Intolerant assessments
Son coiled in classroom corner
Tastes like unchecked bias
Income gap prejudice
Microaggression tainted behavior reports
Feels like strained relationships
Isolation
Village building
Touches like too tight hugs
Food mashed on plates
Pushing to eye contact
Sounds like heart palpitations
Parent protection
Unwrapped gift

Last Dance

coral lipstick stains pillow dents
tears slice two hundred-thread Egyptian cotton
count
her scent saturates mattress
your head rests on lopsided couch

with younger thighs,
I danced for you in bobby socks and peppermint
painted cheerleader's skirt
my heart beating to pace of your glide around the
track for trophies
like me
then, I believed boyhood sincerity

three-year-old vows lodged in our throats
I reach for you like gymnast jammed between
uneven bars
seek cures in camisoles and minis

less blessings in the bank

we once spoke through body language
hips shook on tiled dance floors
eyes fluttered 12 a.m. invitations
knees bent at alter to forgive young love sins

now breasts wilt from weather of neglect
we share occasional joy ride on the backs of
distorted memories
stitches from skirt pull in separate directions
quarrels leave permanent scar tissue

traded law school for spatula
thin waist for babies
childhood version of marriage
for fighting in between silence

crawling to easel,
a painter,
I create mirage

no Tet Offensive
no Malcolm Murder
no children

wild Irish Rose
Marvin Gaye in our souls
smothered in future
past the Cleveland ghetto
to quiet street
where bad habits stay inside

your disappearing act
shreds my illusion
packed boxes swollen in corner

my eyes invite you to stay

we meet at our spot
on olive green rug
covering stained wood

you dig in box for swaying record dipped in dust

wifi spins
we spin in past

don't remember who said what

then cries of our babies wake me
I cradle delicate blessings
no boxes to pack
our home empty for years

Breathless

when nurses told me your due date
10 years after mourning empty womb
wind escaping lungs in whimpered disbelief
turbulence landing on Johns Hopkins airport tarmac
our first road trip together to bury great grandma
you peanut-sized in belly
my excuse for repast fried chicken comfort
potatoes and string bean seconds
cousins wondering where skinny me went

breathless

panting upstairs to corporate job
wondering if spotting
meant more than hormones and life-forming

praying until breathless
and fearless
believing over everything
you were meant to be born
I was built to mother a girl
even when I don't believe I have it in me to do so

breathless

inability to sleep or eat or think
who am I to know how to infuse the self-esteem and
confidence I never had as a child
or a 20-year-old
or even some days now

breathless

calling girlfriends to build me and let me make
mistakes without judging
take risks without fall back plans
live each moment counterintuitively

sitting in its fragility
watching you do these things so much better than
me
days old effortless crawl to nipple to nurse

breathless

when you help your brother remember his epilepsy
medicine
offer to calm him through meltdowns
show him what empathy looks like
when I forget
when daddy forgets
you are so much more than teachers see in
classrooms
or your parents
or any human looking at you through the lens of
their own limitations
calculated consideration of great auntie M
saving pennies for your first home

you believe

planning your own businesses and escape from our
covering

falling and each time starting over
with pro ball player confidence

you are tom boy and princess
docile and powerful
you are moments piled on top of each other
growing heavy on my chest
and every single day
I am
breathless

When Black Girls Go Missing

…Silence.

Motherhood

Reached out with gloom in voice
Waited for you to lift me
Say hair will be on fleek
Offspring will listen when you speak
Visions you had for your future will resurrect
Don't put them to rest yet
But you told me halt slow and wait
Let your mind rest

Til' the last one graduates

Los Angeles

They drive in with loads
Cars sprinting past them on 405
Actors, writers, dancers, directors
Wait tables and bust sudsy inspiration
from brazen customers
Take weekend workshops at UCLA
Form unfunded production companies with cohorts
They drive home empty
When it hurts too hard to stay

Like a Nikki Giovanni Poem

I wish I could be honest
like a Nikki Giovanni poem
'cause I'd tell store grocer
the bag he packed is too heavy for my arthritis
and that parenting hurts
not just a childbirth
but when you place your preschooler on your hip
letting her linger too long
'cause you know she won't want to hang there
next year
I wish I could be honest
like a Nikki Giovanni poem
'cause I'd admit I see myself younger
when I gaze in mirrors
past the grays I never invited
the wrinkles
the gully of fat tissue
the days I know I rushed through
'cause I didn't know better
I wish I could be honest
like a Nikki Giovanni poem
'cause I'd tell you I love you
even when you make me not want to
and I wonder if we fit
or how we got this far
or how we'll make it next year
but that's probably too honest for you.

Resumé

Don't assume you know me
'Cause you caught glimpse of broken dialect
saw my head bang to hip hop cut
You don't know if I'm ego trippin' or code switching
My rhythmic bounce move like confidence
Curled locks lay like new money rains all day
But you have no idea how I got here
Four generations of educated blacks
Our entrepreneurial lineage
don't seep through my hue
Untold stories can't conform
to your version of history

Don't assume you know me
'Cause I pulled out food stamps for bland meal
lingered on bar stools long last night
beat myself up for conflicted thoughts
in hopeless head fight
Master's degree not painted on back
Job lay-off triggers echoed stomach pangs
and sliced esteem
this snap chat of my life doesn't cover my pedigree
I never intended to beg for respect
Or count pennies until my next check
Greater is in me

Don't assume you know me
Lazy, lost, longing for handouts
You assume you know me and my community

Pages of who I am ripped from me

More hidden figures
than a Hollywood movie could capture
Dating back generation, before generation,
before generation
before emancipation
Ancestors built, lost and rebuilt
Settled this very city you occupy
My grandmother planted fruit in Watts
when it was Black and clean
We pressed hairs to assimilate
Practiced Eurocentric diction and perspective
Then witnessed black mens' dreams fade
Like clean water in urban pipes
generation after generation recoil from the weight
of lost civil rights promises
prison pipeline clogging the splintered aspirations
of our children
we built, lost and rebuilt

Don't assume you know me

Ring missing on ring finger
is multiple baby single mama drama
Law degree hung on opulent wall
But purses get clutched when I walk past
My vintage threads speak poverty
'cause I chose to serve my community
in exchange for a higher salary
Don't assume you know me
Question where I grew up
When generation after generation after generation
after 1848 treaty
Placed me on west side

with latte sipping liberals
who think they read my story
in distorted history books
Cinco de mayo solidarity looks
Drunken man kisses Latin fantasy
Underpays staff because we live on less
Cat call Maria, Rosa, Sophia
You don't know if dirt in nails
is from cleaning houses
or cleaning my own
If I rent a place with cousins
If they each own a home

Don't assume you know me
'Cause you hear hint of ethnic dialect
A refuse to fully conform stand
Doesn't make me less American

Don't assume you know me

or you can't be me one day

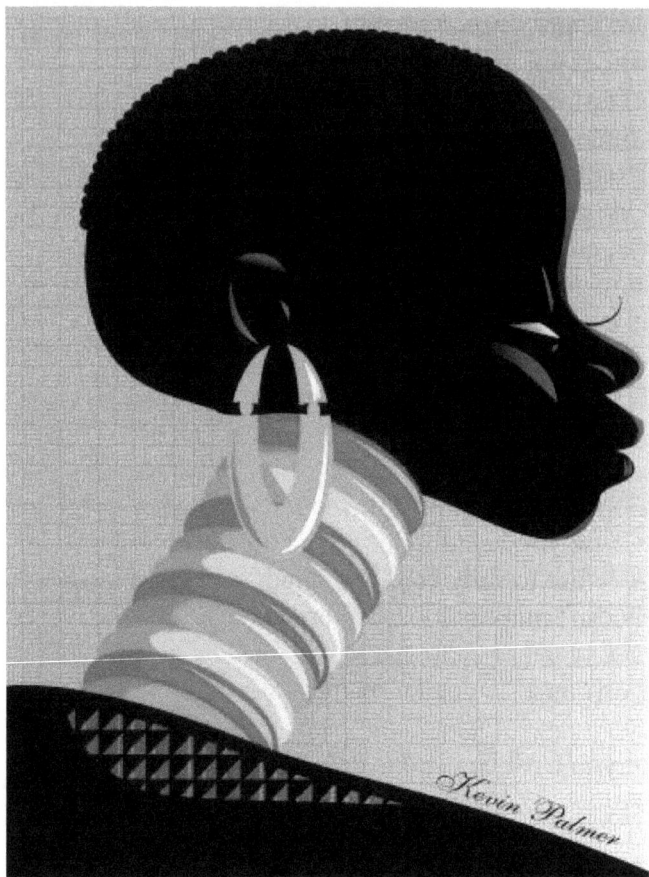

Kevin Palmer

Empty

I miss her
eleven weeks nested in pit
belly bloated quick
plump back drooped in readiness
cramped muscles
muddled memory
dread of inherited blemishes
wrinkled courage layers
too much movement
too early
and blood
and tissue
transfused sobs
leak down cellulite ridges of caramel crusted
wavering thighs
to grey speckled hospital tiles
warmed with her flesh
i settle into empty vessel
she struggled to be here
but we were not ready.

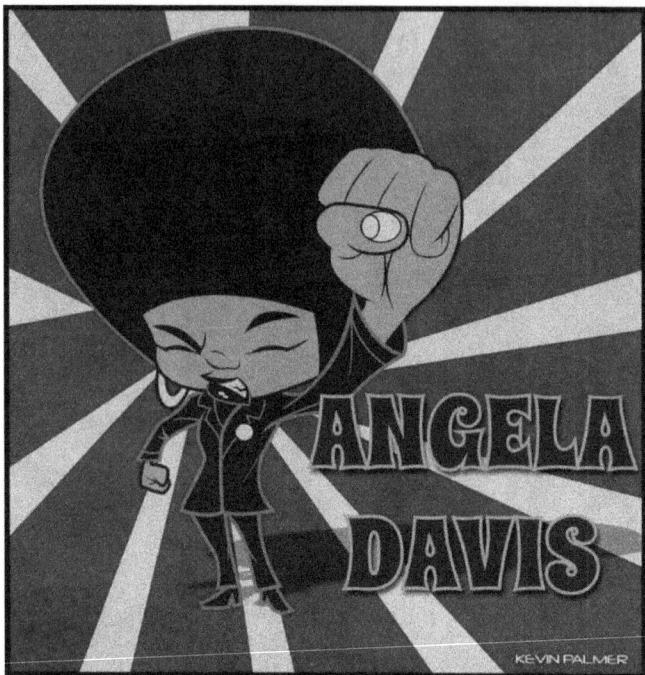

I can't breathe

Emotions forced in corner
Feelings fester on sweat soaked sleeve
Torched hatred on Facebook feed
For perceived privileges
Black bloodlines have yet to receive
ICE raids reign anxiety in son
Form day-mares
during language arts
Carpet time risky
Are they coming for me next?
Inequity so normalized
We wear it like comfortable dog-eared tennis shoes
the ones we refuse to throw away
Rest in it like an abused child
accustomed to twisted love
Unable to envision life absent of oppression
Tastes so familiar
we smell mom's baked sweet rolls
when fed to us
Excuse failings in schools, streets, bank account
We pray through lack
like asking for what is owed is sin
Say what we hear
Angry
Shrink in fear
Indolent
I can't breathe
Bodies of people who look like me, cousins,
brothers, daddy
Pressed in concrete on HD TV
Hoods pulled from closet

Oppression weaved in legislation
Indigenous battle for seats at the back of the bus
Are they coming for me?
Words to comfort my baby ring false
At 6 she peeps twists in fake tongues
Innocence of play taken away
YouTube
Google
Devices in small palms for escape
Now a gate
A path to information overload
in my 6-year-old
Information stripped protection
AND
I
CAN'T
BREATHE

Things End

two years ago
you licked your index finger full of chocolate
vacated from corner of his lip
made me believe in foreverness
not for its perfection
but its authenticity
the love of 60's R&B
and baby making
no words necessary communicating
that shifted to arbitration
leaving dents in what I believe
that never quite restored

Some days

I wish you had hit me
When you had me
Would've known what you were up to
Seen the abuse
Had the good sense to leave you
Hate to admit
Wicked word stains
Still permeate self-esteem
Instead of in God
I trusted in you
Some days
Point-of-view disfigurement
hovers over me
like a thick funk I can't kill
I pray the blessing of my womb
Never meets with your warped nature type
And if she does
foul stench of deceit turns her away
Keeps all matter of men like you at bay
'Cause years later
Some days
I hear things I thought were dead
Disease of insecurity haze my head
I attempt to self-soothe
Manufactured mood
Pretend you no longer exist
I hate to admit
I should be better than this
Even if everything you saw in me was true
Inferior mind and body
Something less than you

My exterior is just a superficial housing
for what the Lord placed in me
though I get off track at times
Doubt I am where I am supposed to be
Those sidesteps cannot replace my Destiny
And I know
You never knew me
Had I sought God in steps
You would have never been a part of me
I thank Him forgiving me
Forgive you not knowing me
Give Him Glory for his Mercy
Bury your words in the grave of my past
I am new thing I was designed to be.

Something New

You called
my insides moved in time
unintentional travel to college campus
conversations
changing world chatter
L train rumbling rhythmically
under snowy clichés
We thought we knew something about something
Shifting side to side in fake fearless
Attempting to fight chi-town winter
Missing my mother's homemade peach cobbler
with biscuit crust
and pretending I could care less about going back
home to Cleveland
or high school gossip
in convenient store parking lot
Your voice moved me to comfort pieces of past
Even still, I know when it is time
for something new

How to Paint A House

Gently apply soothing love strokes
on cracked quarrel corners.
Lovingly patch imperfections.
Caulk cleft walls,
shaped in anger.
Sand grainy surfaces
plastered with in-law interference.
Detect and protect delicate sections.
Bind blistered disappointments
with expectant wallpaper.
Kneel on tarp for forgiveness.
Smooth rough spots with warm words.
Cultivate cohesion with constant prayer.
Strip.
Prime.
And paint again.

Make me a good wife

Make your needs clear as aspen snow
Lie on my nakedness and smother me
with your expectations
Cradle my emotions like fragile newborn
Place your gathered frustrations on my lap
like knitted blanket
Open the dark cavity of your thoughts to me
like erupting volcano
Use your words to heal me
like absolving priest
Protect my vulnerability
like shielding mother
Reach for my needs
like future is wrapped in them
Make me a good wife

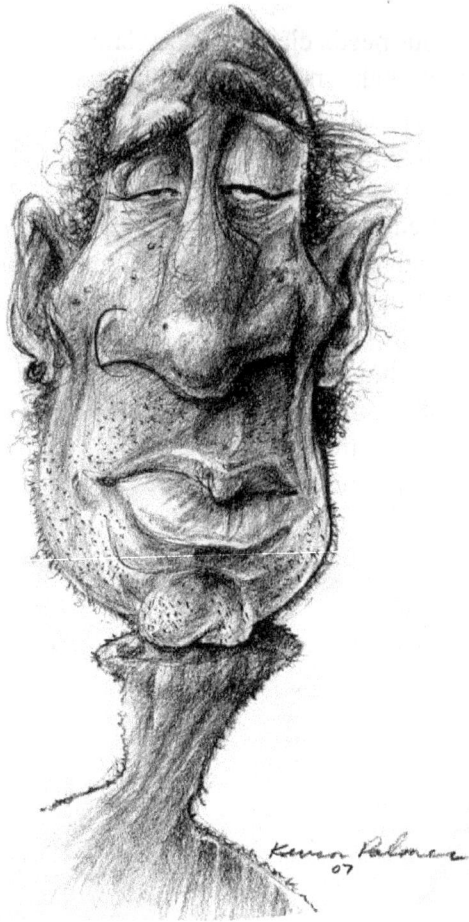

Invisible People

Raid my garbage cans in darkness
Look to restore things I discarded
Reclaim dignity in lightly soiled business suits
And sandals in need of new straps
Race rats for dated meats and bread
Talk to each other and themselves
And by day
Retreat behind freeway signs

Dear 20-something Self

You think he broke you
But you won't know real heartbreak
Until you make a baby with someone you love and
lose her
Or until you bury someone close to you
You will survive these dents
And the transient mistakes
that feel eternal
Though you may never have a best friend again
You will have phenomenal women at each stage of
your life
Who will carry you
And your stuff
And though you don't believe it
No one loves you more than your mother
Even when she picks at little things you do
Or clothes you wear
Or the weight you gained after childbirth
Swears the man she picked for you would've treated
you like royalty
This is how she knows to love
Accept it and your body
The one you think is too skinny to be loved
You may not always have it
Never feel ashamed about going to the small section
in the clothing store
Embrace everything about being young and hopeful
And don't forget who you are
If you even know by now
You don't need anyone's approval to make art

Or to just be
Your life is a canvas
And that is not trite talk
You really can build things from scratch
With the right supports
Identify
Hang on
Be

It is

Cramped finger keyboard pounding
vacuous pats on back
the not yets, not for us, not this season

It is the flirting with Hemmingway martini
digging for Maya Angelou suffering
midnight to morning brain racking

Character voices singing over tinnitus
pushing into dreams day and at night
fall back grad school application rammed in
nightstand

The unbearable waiting like abnormal MRI test call
weighty backload angst
misted eyes of pretend sinus infections

The weeping real
unsureness real
wondering always real

And perversely lonely
and waiting like over-the-counter pregnancy results
but we cannot stop writing

Silent acceptance

quiet girls do not tell
lay when asked
entomb guilt in core
fall in love with predators
give Oscar-worthy accounts of childhood
sit dormant in wood-paneled therapy offices
ideate tv sitcom family
cower from love deep enough to puncture the wall
always protect the assailant

The marrying type

10pm buzz on cell
snap snap of bra
set on eco-friendly bamboo bedding
or maple planked floor
packed Chanel bag of rancid diffidence
Friday nights only
no memorized numbers or nicknames
no sharing of dreams or imagined future
except in my mind
in moments you are mine
knowing in yours
I will never be
the marrying type

Temple of insincerity

some people pray and pretend they don't wonder
never question
never regret
the Moscow mule breath on hymnal singing tongue
the scent of someone they never plan to marry
or the cursing out in the parking lot

when pastors speak repentance
urgent text messages appear on screen
babies need to be changed
hands have to be laid on the grieving neighbor
some people never hear a word for them
and pretend they don't need to

mirrors do not capture indiscretions
scriptures are oddly inapplicable
worship unable to transform
but the pew seat waits for them
in routine expectation
every single Sunday

Downstage

wasn't trying to be funny
not really
sort of
but the aged man in plaid jacket my grandfather
would've worn was not sober enough
to tell the difference between the joke
and therapeutic purging
lights dug in me like trained masseuse fingers
hitting all pressure points
of my struggle with choices and fate
even when I betrayed her
the stage always forgave me
with at least one paunch laugh
from someone who had been where I was
or who could empathize
or both
and no substance on earth
could ever do the same

The Doors

Magnanimous, royal and uncompromising
Safe keeping
Barriers
Paned prophecy entryways
Keys of intent open the doors
You will push, slam, curse them
Strip them
Lay your tiredness on them
Slide in sadness against them
Construct your own doors
Adorn them in petty and purpose
Doors will lock on you
Betray your confidence
Spill secrets with each dent and smudge
Doors will open unexpectedly without effort
Frighten you in their compliance
Capitulate in times when no family nor friend will
The many, many, many doors
Overwhelming in their palm tree presence
You will open doors for others
Discern the doors for you
Craft windows and slither through bars on doors
Lose locked door conflicts
Deconstruct doors
Paint over doors
And one day
You will close your mama's door
Knowing she will never walk out of it
Again

I Know Somebody

I know somebody who would love a few extra
pounds
to get food down
have people tell her she's too round
a few inconvenient whiskers billowing on her lip
extra wide hips
moistness on her mouth
to plant Anastasia orchard purple lipstick
prays to God each time she takes a breath
when he lets her take the next and the next and the
next
too late to do the one day I'll get to them things
revive aspirations she let expire at her office job
dust the pattern leather pumps she put on for the
man who didn't deserve her
would not adore her
too broken to love her
feet too swollen to fit
the seeping through
midnight blue veins
inconsolable joint pain
desperate hanging onto minutes with friends
I know somebody who wants an again
would love a kid who spits up milk
on her maxi dress
keeps her from getting rest
runs in the house to show her an "a" on his test
ignores all of her chore requests
steels her phone and plays video games

snaps photos
breaks things his allowance can't cover
a love that could most likely smother
I know somebody
whose moles, cellulite, figures in her bank
ain't her concern
the degrees on her wall don't illuminate
what she has to learn
to un-plan, un-control, un-analyze her life
value time to the second
as she rehearses the day
her soul takes flight

Pen to Paper

My writing is calm lavender oil
Billie Holiday gut love
Broken first date covenant
Ancestor voices insomnia
Basement greased press and curl to root
Soaked first love pillowcase
Interminable introspection
Immature and seasoned
Southside steppers
Hot sauce on Harold's
Fractured friendships
Death
Life
Therapeutic backyard garden mint leaves
Forest green catholic school girl skirt lifting
Cleveland eastside suburb
Shaw Heights High rivalry
Pop lock and Prince
Needs neither popularity nor profit
Brazen 5 year old tongue
Undaunted by Facebook feed likes
My writing is 48-hour labor pains
Incongruous social justice chants
Superficial platitude
Poetry and stage presence
Healing
Hope
Sunken cry cleansing
Cain Park saucer sled
Cuyahoga River racial divide

Over-sensitive Cancer
80s burgundy cellophane
Mini skirt and LL Cool J
College campus protest rally
Angry
Unforgiving
Rhythmic and off key
Powerful and fragile
Clear muddled mania
Chaotic dogma
Me

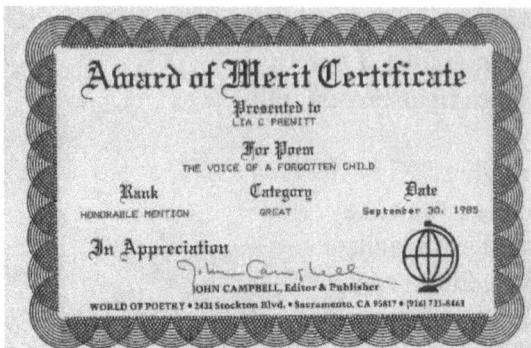

Award of Merit Certificate

Presented to
LIA C PREWITT

For Poem
THE VOICE OF A FORGOTTEN CHILD

Rank
HONORABLE MENTION

Category
GREAT

Date
September 30, 1985

In Appreciation

JOHN CAMPBELL, Editor & Publisher

WORLD OF POETRY • 2431 Stockton Blvd. • Sacramento, CA 95817 • (916) 731-8461

ABOUT THE AUTHOR

Lia P is a mother, wife, advocate and writer who aspires to be a Good Girlfriend.

www.ingramcontent.com/pod-product-compliance
Lightning Source LLC
Chambersburg PA
CBHW062008040426
42447CB00010B/1976